For Michael – your steady presence and playful spirit keep our happy family on track.
S.C

For Laura.
P.C

First published in Australia in 2026 by Affirm Press, a Simon & Schuster (Australia) Pty Limited company
Wurundjeri Woiwurrung Country
Level 3, 162 Collins Street, Melbourne VIC 3000

Affirm Press is located on the unceded land of the Wurundjeri Woiwurrung peoples of the Kulin Nation. Affirm Press pays respect to their Elders past and present.

New York Amsterdam/Antwerp London Toronto Sydney/Melbourne New Delhi
Visit our website at www.simonandschuster.com.au

10 9 8 7 6 5 4 3 2 1

9781923419063 (hardback)

A catalogue record for this book is available from the National Library of Australia

Cover and internal design by Patrick Corrigan
Typeset in Sofia Pro and Auster
Printed and bound in China by RR Donnelley Asia Printing Solutions Ltd

THE SLEEPY TRAIN

Sharna Carter

Patrick Corrigan

Look! Here comes the Sleepy Train.
It's coming, can you see?

All aboard the Sleepy Train
and do the stops with me.

CHOO-CHOO! Bathtime Station.
We wash the muck away.

Splashing bubbles – POP, POP, POP!
It's so much fun to play.

Look! Here comes the Sleepy Train.
Hear the whistle blow.
All aboard and ring the bell.
Chugga-chugga, off we go!

CHOO-CHOO! PJ Station.
Which ones will I choose?

One foot in and HOP, HOP, HOP!
I'm a bouncy kangaroo.

Look! Here comes the Sleepy Train.
Hear the whistle blow.
All aboard and ring the bell.
Chugga-chugga, off we go!

CHOO-CHOO! Brushing Station.
First, I comb my hair.

Toothpaste goes on –
SQUEEZE, SQUEEZE, SQUEEZE!
Then cleaning everywhere.

Look! Here comes the Sleepy Train.
Hear the whistle blow.
All aboard and ring the bell.
Chugga-chugga, off we go!

CHOO-CHOO! Story Station.
I snuggle in my nook.
Turn the pages – FLIP, FLIP, FLIP!
I really love this book.

Look! Here comes the Sleepy Train.
Hear the whistle blow.
All aboard and ring the bell.
Chugga-chugga, off we go!

CHOO-CHOO! Bedtime Station.
I cuddle my bear tight.
Cosy in my blankets,
it is time to say ...

Goodnight.

Shhh! There goes the Sleepy Train.
Try not to make a peep.
It's the Dreaming Station,
and I'm drifting off to sleep.

Choo-choo.